This is dedicated to our Kim – who lived life and showed love, caring and a maturity far beyond her short time with us.

Special thanks:
To my sister, Donnas, who took my ramblings and made them into something readable.

CONTENTS

www.brucewattblog.wordpress.com

INTRODUCTION

My intention in writing this is to offer some exposure of and insight into what happened when a huge and tragic life-changing situation suddenly struck our family. I would like to share the events, awareness, questioning, philosophising, degree of acceptance and level of comfort that have taken place since.

The death of anyone close to you can be a deeply traumatic experience. The loss of a child has to be the most excruciating of all. It seems so unnatural and so out of the correct and expected order of events (despite the many heartbreaking statistics to the contrary) that I have yet to find words to describe it. One can be a widow or widower but there are no words to adequately describe the fact that one has lost a child. Our daughter Kim's diagnosis with cancer and the almost three months we had with her before she left us were life changing. The experience altered our perspectives on daily life, how we interpret life and the hereafter and also how we respond to people and situations.

The most important events in life don't always come with a 'how-to' guide. We had nothing to tell us how to live through and continue to live with what happened to us. If there had been someone to say to us: "I've been down this road; take my hand," it might perhaps have helped.

And that 'perhaps' made me think about writing this book, not only for people who have become 'members of the club that no-one wants to join' but also for family, for friends, for colleagues and carers who would be grateful for some guidance on how to interact with people experiencing this kind of pain.

I hope that the pages which follow provide some idea of what a situation like this puts grieving people through, (No, you are not going crazy!) and, at the same time, offers some insights and helpful direction.

This is essentially a story – a true story with a very sad theme. It is a recount of our experience of grieving. It tells what we lived through and what we felt or couldn't feel. In the story I have tried faithfully to record what happened to us, what we were exposed to and the lessons that we learned.

THE ORDEAL

Picture a reasonably happy, healthy, busy and successful family, living normal lives from day to day with great plans for the future and seeing most of those plans being fulfilled. The career plans of the parents are on track, the house is paid for, the cars also, there is money invested and, generally, everyone's future appears to be secure. The family is settled and the children are now in their upper teens, with all that goes with that. The girls' hormones "have struck" and there are boyfriends and family and friends around. We are lucky in that we have been able to enjoy holidays overseas and the girls are getting a good education.

Then, in three days, our lives changed irrevocably:-

One weekend Kim mentioned that she was feeling stiff and sore and my wife decided that she should go to the physiotherapist for some massage treatment. It was October, just prior to the beginning of Kim's final school exams and everyone in her age group was feeling the pressure.

Monday, 28 October
My wife took Kim to the physiotherapist who examined her and said that she was concerned about some lumps, particularly on Kim's back, that she felt should be investigated further. She contacted our doctor in the practice who examined Kim and also found swollen lymph glands on Kim's neck and under her right arm.

Tuesday, 29 October
My wife took Kim to a specialist surgeon and an ultrasound was done which showed further lesions on her liver and kidneys. The specialist surgeon agreed to do a biopsy the following day.

Wednesday, 30 October
Hospital day - Kim was admitted and the procedure was performed. Afterwards we took her home.

Thursday, 31 October

I received a call from the surgeon who said that he wanted to see me that afternoon. I went in, knowing that this was not going to be good news and, even though I appreciated his candour, I was not prepared for what he told me.

All the results from the biopsies were positive for malignancy and the surgeon told me that, according to his experience, this was a rampant cancer that had taken over Kim's body and brain, probably over the past four to six months, and that the prognosis was bleak. He said that we should work on having Kim with us for the next two months at the most.

I was at a loss as to who to tell about the prognosis. Should I keep this to myself; share it with my wife; share it with the whole family? I just didn't know. I debated long and hard with myself on the drive back home (the first thing that struck me was that, outrageously, the world around me was carrying on as normal – did it not realise that it had tilted completely off its axis?). I finally decided to tell my wife and then we would both decide what to do.

Telling her was one of the hardest things I have ever done (harder things come later) but it was absolutely the right decision. Also, you can't keep too many medical secrets from someone who has been in a pharmacy since childhood and my wife, as a qualified pharmacist, would have a very good idea as to what was happening to Kim when she saw what drugs were being prescribed and the procedures that were to be carried out.

We then spoke to Kim and, as gently as we could, told her that this was a serious situation and that she would need to go through further testing and investigations.

We decided to keep the news from everyone else initially, mainly to keep the situation positive and at least until we had a clearer sense of direction and our emotions had settled. We did eventually share the prognosis with my wife's brother and his wife and also with my sister and this prognosis was something we constantly had at the back of our minds, even when the outlook seemed to appear positive. It was just seventy two hours from Kim's initial visit to the physiotherapist to the prognosis from the surgeon.

Friday, 01 November
We took Kim to an oncologist who ordered an M.R.I. scan which verified the seriousness of what the surgeon had told me and she was checked in to hospital for the weekend and given intravenous steroids to help prepare her for the treatment to come.

What follows is an edited version of the e-mails that I sent out to family, friends and colleagues, once Kim had been diagnosed, to keep everyone updated on her situation. I have left out some of the technical detail.

I hope that this will provide some sense of the great courage shown by our Kim, the wonderful support we enjoyed and the incredible range of emotions that we all lived through – all in the space of just under three months.

Until the final days we never stopped hoping for a miracle and clung to any positive news the oncologist and doctors gave us.

Sent: November 06, 2002

Dear All

I thought that I would give you an update on our Kim after the hectic events of last week - please understand that this is purely for your information and it is up to you as to whether you would like to read this or not.

Kim has Amelanotic Metastatic Melanoma. Big words:-
Amelanotic - the condition has no pigment or colour, so it very difficult - if not impossible - to find the primary infection site.
Metastatic - it has multiplied and spread.
Melanoma - it is a cancer of the skin - in this case it originated in the skin. Sometimes it stays at skin level and sometimes it goes inside the body. In this case it has obviously gone internal.

It is a condition that rapidly spreads through the body and there is no known cure - however, in one percent of known cases there have been spectacular results and total reversals of the condition - nobody knows why!!!

Last week was investigation week and Kim had x-rays, endoscopes and an ultra sound to establish the extent of her condition. She also had three lumps removed which were examined. This culminated in an M.R.I. scan of her brain last Friday.

The truth of the matter is that she has the cancer in her lungs, her kidneys, her liver, her lymphatic system - and her brain. We suspected that things were not right after everything moved so quickly last week and space was made for Kim at every opportunity.

This was all verified last Friday evening when we received the results of the M.R.I. scan and we had a discussion with the oncologist who was very direct and honest - which is what Kim has asked for from the beginning! (wonderful as we don't need to tiptoe around and pretend!!). He told us that he is very worried and he outlined the nature of the cancer and the seriousness of the situation.

This case is extremely unusual in that this kind of melanoma usually hits people who are over 35 years of age and there are very few cases of people below this age. There are also cases where the melanoma has actually started inside the body - usually it is triggered by the sun and the primary site could even be in or behind an eye!

As a result we do not know how the medication is going to affect her. However, the good news is that we have Kim's youth on our side and the oncologist also outlined the plan of action and said that we will fight this as a team with Kim as the leader - whatever she wants, she gets!! Whenever we have a consultation with him the whole family team will be there to discuss what's going on and we are to be open and honest. We will begin by attacking the lesions in the brain and then work our way down the body. What we are aiming for is a remission and, should we reach that, then we discuss the next plan of attack.

So Kim is now at home and we began the immunotherapy on Monday - she takes 3 tablets in the mornings for five days and then we see the oncologist again next Wednesday for tests to see how her body has reacted and how we continue. Please note that the treatment is going to also attack Kim's immune system and, if you have any form of infection - colds, bugs etc. - keep away from anyone who will be going near her as we don't want anything to be transmitted to her which she can't fight!!

The best person through all of this has been Kim herself!! She is being extremely positive, single minded and determined in her purpose to fight this thing and this is at least 90% of the battle. We are also concentrating on the positives and the goals that have been set - one day at a time!! Kim and the rest of us have received the most wonderful and caring support (one girl even offered one of her legs if that would help!!) and we are extremely grateful for the caring, kindness and positivity that has surrounded us.

Thank you for what you have done and your kind thoughts and prayers. What we need right now is the ability to support Kim in her fight and to be there to maintain her incredible courage.

I hope that this gives you a clear enough picture - and, again, many thanks!!

Bruce

Sent: November 15, 2002

Dear All

Thank you all for your interest in Kim and her progress and this is an outline of what has transpired over the past 10 days or so.

I must say that we have been overwhelmed by the kindness, consideration, caring and prayers that she and we have received as a family - thank you!!! Kim has annexed her parent's bedroom as she has a great view of the garden and the river and there is more space for all the flowers and gifts that she has received - and she has a telephone right next to her!!!

She has remained extremely positive and talkative and this is just so encouraging. She has also been most concerned about her friends who are writing Matric at present - or who are about to begin other exams - and she keeps on emphasizing that nobody is to worry about her, she is fighting on!!

We have had visits from numerous friends and family members and also the school Chaplain and the Headmistress. I believe that this has helped keep Kim positive and I also must mention that each class at the school made a card for her and signed it and this pile arrived to Kim's great delight!

So, we took her home last Monday from Pretoria after she spent the weekend at the hospital where her oncologist has beds. She had a catheter port inserted in her upper right chest and it was used over the weekend to give her a strong dose of steroids to reduce the swelling she had, primarily in the brain, and to prepare her body for the chemotherapy. We took the chemo drugs back with us.

Monday evening was not great as we gave her the three tablets to take and there was quite some vomiting - until about 01h00 in the morning. We then consulted with the product manager of the chemo drug (Temoxol) and the oncologist and, since then, we have given Kim her anti-nausea tablet when she wakes in the morning, followed by the chemo tablets a half hour later and then breakfast an hour after that.

Fortunately this has worked and she had her last course on Saturday morning.

She is more pale, she has lost about 2 kilograms and she has the most vivid and weird dreams - she is now taking a sleeping tablet to ensure she has good rest at night. Naturally, she is now considerably weaker and has rested most of the time. We took her to a reflexologist mid last week and this helped - so much so that Kim was very lively for the rest of that day and into the evening. Her uncle Steve also has magic hands and he has been around every morning to give her a massage and to emphasize the positives and get Kim to visualise and concentrate on what she is fighting. She has had days when she has been too tired to see anybody who wishes to visit and please do not feel offended, but understand that she is the team leader and what she says goes!!

To give you an indication of Kim's spirit – last Thursday, she asked us if we should not request that she has a double dose of the chemo in order to hit the cancer harder and quicker!!! It is interesting that she took 300 mg of the Temoxol per day for the five days - the normal full adult dose is 200 mg per day!! Speaking to some medical friends, it also appears that this case is causing quite a stir in medical circles - purely because it is so unusual - and we believe that, under the care of the oncologist and with the interest that this is generating, Kim is receiving the best care possible!!

After a semi restful weekend, mostly with family, (and anybody who has shares in any winery producing Sauvignon Blanc should see a healthy return on their investment in the near future!!) we prepared for the meeting with the oncologist on Wednesday.

What a wonderful anticlimax!!! We went prepared for a battery of tests and scans – the oncologist examined her and pronounced that she is responding extremely well to the treatment - there are no new lumps and the existing ones appear to be shrinking and becoming softer!! Fifteen minutes after we went in, we walked out - with our jaws still hanging open!!

We are by no means out of the woods - but we do have an extremely positive start and a good base to work from. Now it is a case of building up Kim's immune system with the right foods and trying to get some more weight back on to her body and we see the oncologist again in two weeks time - this time there will be more extensive blood tests.

We now have a frightening array of healthy foods in the house and I am sure that the family's eating habits will be changing somewhat over the next months - hey, whatever it takes!!!

To everyone who has been behind Kim in this, thank you for all you have done so far - she (and we) feel surrounded by a wonderful bubble of support and please keep the positivity coming. We have successfully passed the first hurdle and now we need to maintain the momentum and build on the first glimmer of light that we have seen in the last two weeks or so.

Thank you again!!!

Bruce

Sent: November 24, 2002

Dear All

This, I think will be comparatively short as we have had a fairly uneventful time since my last e-mail. I would, however, like to thank all who have also shown concern for us as a family. I think that we have more or less come to terms with the reality of the situation and have generally handled it well - with the odd "wobbly" every now and then.

I think that we are fortunate in that we said right at the beginning that we were not going to embark on any guilt trips, nor enter into any debates with God - and I believe that it has given us a solid base.

My wife is frustrated that there is not more that she can do - given her pharmaceutical background - and is very keen to put weight onto Kim as soon as possible in preparation for the next chemo session. The health food route is OK but Kim's weight is still fluctuating and tending towards down. Also, Kim's insulin levels climbed very high two days ago, which gave us some concern. My wife has spoken to the oncologist and he has basically said that she can give Kim whatever she likes (given certain restrictions) as her pharmacy background will dictate good sense. This includes supplements - which we thought was a: "no, no!!" - so it will be interesting to see what develops over the next few days.

Kim's sister has tended towards being quiet and she likes to get out of the house every now and then. I think that she has handled herself extremely well and remains very supportive and positive. It is also good that she is back at school and just about finishing her exams.

I am pleased that I have the opportunity to be back at work - sitting and dwelling is not good for me!!

The word of Kim's situation has really spread and we have had encouragement, support and prayers, not only from around the country, but from all over the world - Australia,

England, Canada, Singapore, Zimbabwe, Malawi, Kenya and New Zealand. Thank you all!!!

Kim is still pale and skinny but remarkably perky (I shudder to think of what our 'phone bill is going to be!!) and should you wish to see her please may I ask two things:-
- If you have any form of infection, please do not even think about it - her resistance is too low.
- If you would like to come and see her, please 'phone first as there are times when she is tired and just wants to rest - or sleep.

This week had two lows and two highlights:-

The first low was our concern about the rapid rise in the insulin levels - fortunately sorted out rapidly.

The second is that Kim absolutely refuses to mow the lawn!!

The first highlight was on Wednesday evening when our domestic help for the last 18 years brought her prayer group to the house to pray for Kim. The session went on for just over half an hour and it was extremely touching.

The second was when we went as a family to visit a special family yesterday. They have two girls at St Mary's School and the father has been battling Hodgkin's Disease - Lymphatic Cancer - for the last 10 years or so. He (and his family) have been through the mill - but he's still around!! The father was wonderful in putting the whole thing into perspective. One daughter outlined her feelings, which was great for our younger daughter - and the mother gave some very realistic feelings from a mother and wife point of view. What came through was really positive and unselfish and I think it helped us tremendously in that we could see the day to day reality of living with cancer as opposed to visualising various (and usually depressing) scenarios. The father put it extremely well when he said that we all have problems in our lives - and Kim's big one has just arrived somewhat early and her life is going to change. But we all handle our problems and we all get on with living!! I believe it was extremely beneficial to us all and a big "Thank You!!" to such a brave family!! *(The father lost his battle in July 2006 and we were privileged to be able to attend the funeral of such a great fighter!)*

We see the oncologist on Wednesday after some tests and hopefully he will give us further direction and we will do our best to feed Kim up before that!!

We'll keep in touch!

Bruce

Sent: November 28, 2002

Dear All

It was a fairly quiet and apprehensive car as we drove to Pretoria yesterday for Kim's blood tests and consultation with the oncologist.

We arrived, Kim had her tests and we were shown into the oncologist's rooms. After asking the standard questions about Kim's energy levels, eating habits, weight etc. he took us into his small examination room to see how Kim had progressed. It was interesting to see his eyes grow bigger as he felt around her neck for some of the lumps. He prodded and poked around for a bit longer and then asked us to go back to his office.

When we sat down he had a smile on his face, he raised his fists into the air and said a very quiet but vehement: "Yessss!!!" He said that he is thrilled with the progress and that whatever we are doing, keep on doing it!! He said that we now know we have a direction and Kim needs to get on with life and handle situations as they arise.

So much so that he strongly encouraged Kim to go to the coast this Friday for the post Matric Exams madness week - where the place is taken over by a horde of 18 year olds, celebrating the end of the Matric exams and their school careers!! This despite the fact that Kim will be starting her next course of chemo next Monday. We collected the drugs before returning to Johannesburg.

So, we will drop Kim at the airport early tomorrow for her flight to the coast and then we will drive down. We have accommodation nearby and our aim is to be unobtrusive and out of the way - but around if necessary.

Kim knows what she can and cannot do and can and cannot eat (and drink!!) and the friends she is sharing a room with are great girls!!

I will fly back home on Monday afternoon, then my wife and other daughter will drive back and Kim will fly back on Thursday.

This means that we will be ready for the final assembly at the school next Friday, December 6 - which is to be preceded by a special service for Kim - amazing thoughtfulness!! It was also amazing to hear the oncologist tell us that Kim is his most popular patient ever and that we have to have the most incredible support base as he is asked about Kim by so many people.

Thank you God, thank you Uncle Steve for the amazing time you have spent with Kim with your massaging and healing therapy and thank you to everyone for the continuing support and positivity!!! Yesterday was indeed an emotional day because now we can dare to hope - and Kim is still there leading the charge!!! (She mentioned yesterday that she would like to be a volunteer counsellor for children who have just been diagnosed with cancer!!)

Our next appointment with the oncologist is on December 11 and he wants a chest x-ray, in addition to the usual blood tests - interesting that the nagging cough Kim had for the past couple of months is no longer!!!

We'll let you know how we go!!!

Bruce

Sent: December 13, 2002

Dear All

I believe that e-mail protocol dictates that you should not type anything in capitals as it means that you are shouting at the recipient. In this case - tough - KIM IS IN PARTIAL REMISSION!!!!!

We went to Pretoria on Wednesday, they took blood, Kim had her chest x-ray and we went into the oncologist's office. Again, he asked the usual questions, felt around a bit and then he looked at the x-rays. He said he has had results, he has had good and really good results - but Kim's progress has been spectacular!!

He (and we) could not believe the progress that Kim has made over the last 5 weeks since the first diagnosis was made. I looked over my first e-mail to you all before writing this and the difference really is incredible!
We looked at the difference between the first and the recent x-rays and, where there were three lesions, there is now a fraction of only one left. At a calculated estimate, 80% of the cancer in the areas that we are currently concentrating on (not the brain etc.) has gone!!!

There is also an enzyme in the liver (L D H Enzyme) that encourages cancer growth. Kim's initial level of this enzyme was 1100 - it is now down to 300 and the level we are aiming for is 230!

The oncologist was also extremely honest when he said to us that, if Kim had not responded in the way she has, we would be checking her in to Hospice at this time - it really was that serious!!

I believe that we have been witness to a miracle and that we can now begin to hope for a life for our daughter!!! The oncologist said that this is a strange and cunning disease and nothing is predictable, but, given Kim's progress to date, there is definitely room for hope of a full remission.

The treatment is working and he has a direction and we see how we progress from here. He has not looked at her brain yet as, apparently, this takes a long time to heal / recover and this is obviously a cause for continued concern - but - this latest news is the best Christmas present we have ever received!!!

I think it has been the most exhausting time of our lives and we are still feeling somewhat shell-shocked, but, again, the support we have enjoyed has been so wonderful. We went to the school last Friday before their last assembly where they had arranged a special service for Kim in the chapel, with the Matric girls and the staff that were able to attend. It was a moving, emotional and light-hearted experience and a very big "Thank you!" to Mrs. Fargher (the Headmistress), Father Bailey and all who made this possible. The most special part was when everyone went up individually and lit small candles from the big central candle on the altar and placed them around it - a memory we will hold forever!!

Thank you also to everyone who has kept up their support and positivity - in whatever way it is coming through to Kim - it is working!!!!

We have the next dose of chemo which Kim will begin between Christmas and New Year and we are all looking forward to a comparatively relaxing family Christmas - maybe we will even get our bedroom back!!. Kim then sees the oncologist early next year and I will keep you updated.

From all of us - thank you - we feel very full at the moment and really appreciate the support we have all received. Please keep it up and we wish you a healthy and very happy festive season!!

Watch this space in 2003!!

Bruce

Sent: January 03, 2003

Dear All

Well, 2003 has arrived and I do hope that everyone had a restful, peaceful and enjoyable festive season - and that the year ahead holds good things for us all, wherever we are!!!

This e-mail is a bit early but the reason is that we need plenty more positivity and prayers, please. We unfortunately did not have a good Christmas and our Kim is not in a good way at the moment!!

Just before Christmas she complained of pain between her shoulder blades to the right of her spine. She was also not eating and bringing up most of what she did get down. There was also a dry cough, a lot of listlessness and she spent a lot of time sleeping. Thankfully her spirit was still great.

We got concerned and checked the chemo drug's information insert and some of these symptoms did apply. However, my wife still took her to one of the oncologist's locums (he is on holiday until Jan 06) who agreed that Kim was suffering side effects of the chemo. Thank God I have a pharmacist for a wife as she was not happy and pressed for further investigation.

We then went to see another oncologist - who took x-rays and then started moving. He was very concerned, said there was fluid in the right lung cavity and, this last Monday, we admitted Kim to the Flora Clinic. Kim was so dehydrated that they could not operate on the Monday and they inserted a drip to replace her electrolytes and re-hydrate her.

On Tuesday morning the thoracic surgeon operated on Kim and drained 4 litres of fluid from the lung cavity!! He inserted a drain and also did a biopsy of the lung, the fluid and the thymus (lymph) gland. Kim has now drained a little under 5 litres of fluid from the cavity - just over 10 percent of her body weight!!!!

Some backhanded good news is that the pathology of the fluid in the lung itself shows no malignancy - this is the lung that had three big tumours in it. However, the big problem is the thymus gland, which is located just above the lungs, under the breastbone. This is very malignant and inflamed and swollen - to such an extent that it is blocking air access to the right lung (and probably prevented Kim from keeping any food down as well).

As a result, her right lung has collapsed and there is big concern over this and the malignancy and swelling of the thymus.

So, Kim is now in Intensive Care at the Flora Clinic and she began radiation treatment on the thymus gland area yesterday. She has had two treatments, will have a break over the weekend and then three more from Monday onwards. The Intensive Care staff are very competent and very serious - immediate family only and only two at a time. There is also no visiting outside of the designated hours and we have to wash our hands before we touch her!!

She is obviously very weak and somewhat spaced out on the morphine she is being given. Intensive care is also an unsettling experience for us and it has obviously been a pretty intense time for the family as well. Fortunately Kim was today moved to a private glassed off area in the ward as another patient was moved out and the hospital staff are extremely concerned about any form of infection she might pick up as her resistance is so low. It is not a great sight seeing her lying there with a mass of tubes and monitors feeding her and recording her vital signs!!

My big concern is for her spirit - I know it is dulled by the morphine but this is the main reason for this e-mail. Please send her as much as you can in the way of positivity and good prayers - we really will appreciate as much as we can get!!!

We are deeply worried but cautiously optimistic – the oncologist did say that this is a cunning disease and it has just shown its' true colours. This was one area that was clearing so well and now it has just flared up!! We are going from hospital visit to hospital visit and it's one day at a time. The next big day will, I think, be when the radiation is completed and they do tests again - mid to late next week.

I will keep you updated and please keep the good stuff coming!!!!!!

Bruce

At this point, feelings of utter helplessness, total frustration and a fair degree of anger really came to play in my emotions.

My gut instinct was saying, "I am the head of the family. I am supposed to be in control and make things happen and fix situations." But here was something that I could do absolutely nothing about!

I remember telling a couple of people that if someone had said lifting a car with my bare hands would cure Kim, I'd have done it, no question. But, instead, I had to try to accept that nothing I could ask of myself would make any difference at all. Nothing!!

Sent: January 16, 2003

Dear All

I am typing this with a very heavy heart as, unless we have a major miracle, the prognosis for Kim is bad. However, let me first update you on events since my last e-mail.

Kim completed her radiation at the Flora Clinic and remained in intensive care until the oncologist arrived back from his leave. He was shocked to hear of the situation as we were all so buoyant the last time he saw her. He first spoke with the relevant Flora Clinic doctors and then met with us.

We asked for it straight and got it straight - Kim's condition is terminal, the chemo and the radiation has not worked and he was very concerned about Kim's quality of life and comfort. I asked him if there is anything further that could be done - use an endoscope and put a tube into her where the growth is blocking the entrance to the lungs / drain the tumour / operate and cut the tumour out / more chemo???? He said that anything like what I suggested would kill her as she is so weak.

We then discussed the options and decided to ask Kim if she would like to go back to Pretoria - which thankfully she readily agreed to. Please understand that we were very happy with the doctors, staff and facilities at the Flora Clinic, but Kim has a special bond with 'her' oncologist and this was proven over the next days.

So, on Friday last, we put her into an ambulance with us following on the ride to Pretoria where Kim was checked into the room next to where she was initially. She was exhausted and found it difficult to get comfortable after the journey but happy to be at The Little Company of Mary Hospice.

The oncologist literally bounced in to the room on his rounds, welcomed Kim back, said it was good to see her and that she had far too many pipes and goodies sticking out of her and they were going to begin reducing all her attachments. He said she has to begin eating and exercising and he would then begin more treatment once she was out of bed for at least 50% of the day. Just the tonic that Kim needed and she responded beautifully - her fight returned and she is positive all over again.

The next day, fortunately, there were very few visitors as the effects of the transfer the day before, the change of environment from I.C.U. to a normal room and having an enema took their toll severely. She was absolutely exhausted and slept for virtually the entire day. We became extremely worried about her skin pallor - so much so that we spent the night in Pretoria – my wife in the room with Kim and me in the car (I am told that I am one of the noisiest sleepers in South Africa!!!!). I really thought that this was "check out" time for Kim!!!

Sunday dawned, we went home to freshen up and returned to a chirpy and perky Kim about 3 hours later. We still spent that night in Pretoria but have been home every night since. The most important thing is that Kim has her fighting spirit back and is prepared to soldier on. Her bond with the oncologist is amazing and he is the most superb psychologist, in addition to his other excellent talents. He has put her on to a small dose of chemo once a week and this has also helped her psychologically.

The physiotherapist arrives twice a day and Kim really tries to do her exercises and she is also trying to eat. We have scoured the restaurants in the area for menus and we then go and get whatever lunch and supper she feels like.

They have taken out all her pipes and tubes, with the exception of the oxygen and her drip, and she is more comfortable and is sleeping much better. What she cannot understand is why she is so tired all of the time and she is frustrated that she cannot be up and about and fighting on.

We spend our days and evenings in Pretoria and return home once Kim has been settled for the night. Last night Kim managed a bath and felt a whole lot better and ready for a good sleep afterwards.

Kim does not know this (AND MUST NEVER KNOW!!!!!!) but the oncologist has intimated that he feels Kim has up to three weeks left. We met with a lovely Hospice person yesterday and Kim's sister will be seeing her again. She has displayed the most amazing maturity and competence and she really has tried so hard - she even tried ironing some of our clothes when our domestic servant was on leave!!! – but, she is battling with the reality now and will need the help that Hospice can provide.

The emotional roller coaster that we have been on has been tiring and the events of the past days are a bit hazy, but I think that this is an accurate enough picture. We can only have immense admiration for our new friend who is fighting Lymphoma with his family who have been riding a similar roller coaster for the last ten years since he was diagnosed as terminal!!

I would really like to thank all the staff at work who have carried on so well through all of this - you are a special bunch!!!

Also, "Thank you" to my wife's clients who have been so understanding!!

Lastly, "Thank you" to everyone who has provided so many forms of support in so many ways - we all do feel very special!!

Kim is fighting, and please remember that visits with her must be short as she tires quickly - if she starts closing her eyes, it is her polite way of saying: "Please leave now!!"

Miracles can happen and we are still hoping and hanging in there!!!

Bruce

Sent: January 26, 2003

Dear All

You might have been aware that, just for a moment, the world stopped at 21h45 on Thursday 23 January when our Kim left us quietly and with dignity.

The funeral is to take place at St Mary's School in Burn Street in Waverley this coming Tuesday at 16h00.

Please can we ask that we do not receive any flowers or other thoughtful gestures - we already have been overwhelmed by kindness and, after having discussed this with the school, please would you rather make a contribution to the school bursary fund - now to be known as the Kim Watt Bursary Fund. We are very keen and hopeful that this fund will provide other girls with the opportunity of experiencing the same caring and nurturing educational environment that our girls have enjoyed:-

Kim Watt Bursary Fund
St Mary's School
P O Box 981
Highlands North
2037
South Africa

If you did not see the article about Kim in Friday's *Star* newspaper, please allow us to be proud parents for a while and give you her Matric exam results:-

Art .... B
English .... Distinction
Afrikaans .... Distinction
Maths .... Distinction
Biology .... Distinction
Geography .... Distinction

They unfortunately left out the Guts and Determination result - but we know what she got!!!

I know in my last e-mail that I said that Kim should not know the length of time she had to live; however, her condition deteriorated severely towards the end of that week and we decided to talk to her. This was really for two reasons:-

- The hospital staff had removed all the pipes and tubes and this was really so that her system would slowly shut down and, when they took the saline drip out, this was a clear signal to us. Kim then was only on the oxygen.
- We were concerned that Kim might have some unfinished business that she wanted to see through - and we wanted her to have an opportunity to take care of this.

So - together with the head nurse and a social worker who gave a very gentle official version of the outcome - we spoke to her as a family and said that the oncologist had always said that she was in charge - now she was in supreme charge and she could have or do whatever she wanted. If she wanted to go home, she could - if she wanted to jump out of an aeroplane, she could - if there was anybody she wanted to see, we would bring them. This was one of the hardest moments of our lives and extremely emotional.

Kim, however, said that she was going to keep on fighting and beat this thing - and she did fight, right until the end!!! We, as a family discussed this afterwards and agreed that we did the right thing at the right time - particularly as Kim has always wanted the truth.

After this the three of us spent every night at the hospital and Kim's condition deteriorated rapidly. Even though the physiotherapist tried, she was unable to walk, was battling to breathe and eventually could not move her legs. She had one position she was comfortable in and was extremely unhappy if we tried to move her. So the morphine doses increased until she was in no pain and felt comfortable. The oncologist saw her on Monday and we mentioned that there was also swelling in her lower abdomen area. He examined her and said that the following morning they would do an M.R.I. scan to pinpoint the areas of fluid build-up and then remove the fluid with a syringe. He then saw her on the Tuesday morning and said that they were not going to do anything as Kim was just too weak and he felt that she was entering her 'final stage'!!

On Saturday Kim twice mentioned her best friend Cathy who moved to Australia two years ago - her polite way of saying she would like to see her!! On Sunday morning I 'phoned Australia and Cathy got on to a flight which arrived here on Tuesday evening. To Cathy's parents - thank you for allowing your daughter to come - to see the smile on both their faces when they saw each other made it all so worthwhile. Kim was weak and did not have a good day on Tuesday and I was seriously worried that Cathy would not make it in time - but Kim managed to lift her arms and give Cathy a hug when she saw her.

Kim then sat with her boyfriend, Cathy and two other school friends and was perky for about a half hour before we prepared her for sleep. Cathy and my wife spent the night in the room and Kim's sister and I were lucky enough to sleep in the hospital counselling room.

After Kim saw Cathy and her friends, it tended to be downhill from then on. It was amazing that the nurses who were not going to be back on duty until the weekend all came in to see us and Kim (they knew - but the fact is that they made the effort to say goodbye.) Kim slept most of the time and hardly spoke unless it was to ask us for something to drink or to make her more comfortable.

On Thursday morning her breathing was an effort and she could hardly speak.

In the afternoon she was sleeping, with my wife and her sister dozing in the room when she began talking.

I went in and Kim grabbed me with an incredible strength and said that I must make the person at the bottom of her bed go away as she didn't want to go (fighting to the end!!!).

I held her and said I would do that – but that that person was waiting to be with her and help her on her new and wonderful journey. My wife and other daughter also held Kim and spoke to her and told her that it was time to go, that it was alright to go and that she should look out for all the pets she'd had over the years.

The Hospice staff heard the commotion and came in to the room and offered to help. We told them to please wait. This was something momentous happening!

After about thirty seconds Kim then said: "Am I back? Am I back?" and relaxed.

She had more medication and was sedated and she then dozed off.

Those were the last words that she spoke and, as she lay quietly, I was able to stretch her out on her back and there was no objection from Kim at all, whereas, just before this, lying on her side in a semi foetal position was the only way she could be comfortable.
If it is possible to describe Kim at that stage, she looked totally at peace and beautiful with a skin like porcelain.
We 'phoned her friends and family and they all arrived, together with the school Chaplain - through the most appalling traffic conditions - thank you all!!! The four of us had a short prayer session with the Chaplain and then everyone else joined us for further prayers. Thank you Father for being there at exactly the right time and for being able to release Kim - she needed that!!

A few of us stayed behind and Kim then quietly slipped away at a quarter to ten.

We did decide to donate whatever of Kim's organs would be useful and both her corneas were harvested. Again, wonderful people, they 'phoned to say thank you, 'phoned again to tell us that the corneas were perfect, and then again to tell us that the first cornea had been successfully implanted on Friday morning.

Thank you Kim's oncologist - you are an incredible, knowledgeable, caring and compassionate man. We loved the way you handled our situation.

Thank you to the staff at The Little Company of Mary Hospice - we could not have asked for better care. You always went the extra mile to ensure that Kim (and the rest of us) were comfortable and well looked after.

Thank you God?? Not quite yet - I think I want to kick your shins first!!!

Have we learned anything from all this?:-

Kim's influence on people's lives has been considerable and her life and disease has touched the lives of so many others and hopefully has helped (and will help) others with the same condition in the future.

A solid family unit is one of those things that are just meant to be - we would not have made it through this ordeal as unscathed as we have if we did not have each other.

Family is so important - every single member of our immediate families has been around at some stage - and also known when not to be around!! Guys, your contribution and support was invaluable - thank you!!!

A caring and nurturing school environment is vital for a complete education - and, boy, have we just experienced this!! Thank you so much Meg Fargher, Father Bailey and all at the school for all your support and for the honour we feel in having the final ceremony in your company.

True friends are always true - thank you to all of you for all you have done - we feel very full when we think of it all!!!

Our city does have a soul!!

I have one final request before ending this - and it is a sincere one!!!

Please, please do not grieve for Kim!!! Miss her, think about her, laugh about her, debate about her, argue about her - but please release her to embark on her journey to be with her angels, unhindered by regrets or any other 'baggage'. She deserves that from us.

Thank you all for sharing this experience with us!!

Bruce

AN ESSAY FROM KIM'S SISTER

Losing her sister was obviously devastating for our other daughter and she vented her feelings in an essay that she wrote, describing what she witnessed and her feelings on the day Kim left us – very brave for a 16 year old!

THAT'S NOT FAIR

I am woken by a gentle kiss on the forehead. With my eyes still closed I hear a soft: "It's time to go baby." from my Mom. The time is half past five in the morning and the continental pillows which I have made my bed are hardly underneath me as I feel the hard cold of the hospital floor against my back. I suddenly remember where I am and, like every morning for the last week, I listen for her breath. She is still breathing.

I kiss her and tell her I love her - just in case I do not get to tell her later. With eyes still closed, she smiles at me.

My parents and I go home to freshen-up and repack the cooler-box and I notice immediately that there is a silent urgency in the atmosphere today, but it is even more than before. A panic, something between the three of us that is unspoken yet understood, seems to have replaced the air around me.

The half-hour road trip back to the hospital seems to take forever and I find myself holding my breath. When we finally arrive back on our balcony outside her room it is half-past nine and I am wide awake with my heart thumping in my chest. I trip over the leg of a chair in my rush to see her, to see if she is still here and she smiles at me as I stand by her bed.

Throughout the morning she occasionally opens an eye or nods her head to answer a question, she is very tired and soon falls back to sleep quickly. As I sit holding her hand the afternoon creeps closer and the bubbles from her oxygen tank are loud in the silence of this room.

I look at the clock. It is three o'clock and she is lying on her side facing me. She starts to stir and shake her head. Frowning, but still quite gently, she says: "No!" Is she dreaming? I stand awkwardly beside her, not knowing what to do or how to comfort her. The tone in her voice and her facial expressions become desperate. She is afraid: "No! No! No!"
What do I do? How can I make her not feel scared? I do not want her to be scared.

My Mom and I call my Dad out of panic and desperation because she is getting worse and will not respond to anything we say. Her eyes are still closed and she is now pleading: "No, I don't want to! No!" Her eyes fling open. They are so wide and so blue, blue like I have never seen them before, but she is not looking at anything specific. Her eyes, completely glazed over, dart frantically around the room. She starts tugging at my Dad's shirt saying: "Take him away! I don't want him here!"

Desperate to comfort her, my Dad surrounds her with his arms. She is terrified and starts pointing next to the bed with strength we have not seen in a month. She says that "he" is there, that there is someone trying to take her away.

My eyes fill with hot tears, which start streaming down my face, and now my eyes are wide too. In this moment I would do anything to take away her fear and make her feel safe again, to bring her back, but I just stand there, dumb and helpless.

My Dad assures her: "He's going. I'm taking him away, he's going away." Her whole body relaxes and her eyes half close. Her breathing is sharp and shallow now and she sounds and looks exhausted.
It is a quarter past three and time to call the family.

The feelings that follow those words are gushing around my stomach and form a lump in my throat. I am completely numb. Everyone is quiet. She is calm now as I sit staring at her, waiting for her to wake up.

I hear my Dad say that Father Bailey is on his way and the nurse smiles at me. It is a sympathetic, loving smile and I see a message in her eyes. A message that says: "I'm so sorry." She turns around and leaves.

With Father Bailey and the family, we all join hands in a circle around the bed and say a prayer. My face is wet and I cannot take my eyes off her. Then sitting by her bed, I watch each of my family whisper a personal something in her ear and then leave.

It is now just me, my parents, my uncle and aunt, and Father Bailey. We are all sitting as close to the bed as possible, as to gently hold at least one place on her. I am holding her hand.

It is now my turn. I walk round to the other side of her bed, where it is easier to reach her, and I quietly thank her for being my sister and I tell her that I love her. With the painful question in my mind of whether she could hear me and whether she knows that I wish I had said it more often, I give her a kiss on her warm, slightly wet forehead and return slowly to my seat.

An hour passes and she is breathing once a minute now, I know we have all been counting. My Mom turns to me and starts to say something but she soon stops. It is a quarter to ten and, after what seems like ages, she says: "I haven't heard a breath for a while."

My Dad slowly gets up and feels her neck and chest. He looks at us. He turns to her and gently closes her eyes, gives her a kiss and says: "Goodbye Kimmy-Kim". My chest feels so tight, like someone is trying to squeeze the breath out of me, and my eyes burn with tears. A feeling of desperation surges through me and I feel like a young child, as if something has been snatched away from me, but as the adult I know I can never have it back, never touch it or enjoy it again. My cloudy eyes search for my Mom because I need to be held, not just by anyone, I need my mother.

While we wait outside the nurses come in to change and cover her. They do not cover her completely, just to below her neck.

I soon return to a dim, quiet room. She lies silently, bathed in a soft yellow light. Her forehead is cold as I give her one last kiss, the last kiss I will ever give her.

SINCE KIM'S PASSING

Right after Kim left us we had absolutely no idea of what we were doing.

Numb! Numb! Numb!

It was like living with a chaotic mental paralysis:-

What to do?
What to say?
How to behave?
When to eat?
What to think – how to think?

We just didn't know!!

And time seemed to pass so slowly and yet so quickly.

This was an enormous thing to cope with, to try to understand and to come to terms with. The new reality, trying to get to grips with the loss, wondering what we should be doing next, what we should be thinking and feeling, and more, had us all feeling surreal and disoriented.

As the days slid by, we gradually regained contact with the world around us.

The week after the funeral I went back to work – often a male way of handling traumatic situations and, for me, it was a case of getting back into a situation that is consistent, day to day and an indication of normal life.

The company I was with had been extremely supportive since Kim's diagnosis and they continued to be so. With the emotions I was experiencing my sleeping hours were not regular and there were times when I would arrive at work exhausted and would fall asleep at my desk or even during meetings. The office or meeting room door would be quietly closed and I would be left to sleep. When I woke up it was business as normal and we would carry on. Nobody asked questions, particularly deep ones and I was not given a time by which I had to be recovered and healed – how can anyone impose these kinds of rules anyway, particularly if they have not been through something similar? The acceptance and support of all those at work was remarkable and I do believe that it was a great help in keeping me on track and, over some months, being able to operate comparatively normally.

We all had individual and some group counselling with some very special people at the South African Chapter of a worldwide self help organisation called The Compassionate Friends, a Non Profit Organisation with a wonderful group of people who have all lost children and who counsel others in the same situation once they have managed to come to terms with their own loss. They helped us immeasurably with our own perspective and coping – there is nothing like talking with someone who has been there!

Almost two years after Kim's passing I, in my turn, was asked to give a presentation at The Compassionate Friends. I talked about some of the thoughts and experiences I'd written down during those first months of our bereavement. I'm proud to say my talk was well received and it forms the basis of a letter that we now send, when we feel it is appropriate, to other people who have recently lost a child. More about that letter later on.

I also gave a second presentation at a Compassionate Friends evening dealing with 'Men and Grieving' because a man's way of dealing with loss is so often different from a woman's. More about this subject, too, later on.

In addition to being an experienced pharmacist, my wife is a great care giver and it seems as though there have been certain customers who have 'found' her at the pharmacy. Yes, it is the nature of the job and looking at a doctor's prescription does give the pharmacist a very good idea as to the condition of the patient, but there have been too many people who will only deal with her and who say that they were meant to see her and that she has been so helpful. There have also been so many cases where she has filled scripts for customers who have a relative or, particularly, a child who is seriously ill or who has just died. This has enabled her to give understanding, compassionate and meaningful advice and, on some occasions she (with me with her when required) visits the patient and family, dispensing further help and sharing the wisdom she has gained.

HOW WE HAVE BEEN AFFECTED

Naturally this has been an enormous life changing experience – we will never be the same again and our perspective on life has changed considerably. The way that we now live our lives is more thoughtful and our interaction with people now involves far more consideration for the circumstances and points of view others may have. We respond to day to day situations and decisions in a more carefully considered way now. I believe that these changes have been for the right reasons and we are better people as a result.

We now find that we're happier living a quieter life; that we're less reliant on the company of others and that social chit chat for the sake of it has little place in our lives. Our outlook has also changed in that we prefer to concentrate on things that are positive and people who are the same. This perfectly supports the adage: "It's not what you say, it's the way that you say it".

As strange as this may seem, our biggest realisation has been that we were exceptionally lucky to have had time to spend with Kim. People often cannot understand how we can say this as Kim's last two and a half months was incredibly uncomfortable for her and emotionally bewildering and draining for us.

But we had time with her. Just as people have difficulty understanding what the loss of a child involves, I cannot comprehend what it would be like to have been contacted by someone and informed that Kim had died suddenly as the result of some accident or violent incident.

As difficult as it was, we had the opportunity to say "Goodbye", to Kim and to release her and help send her on her way. This was a privilege that words cannot describe.

During the last few weeks that we had with Kim we were able to learn more about her and the influence that she had on the people around her. Teenagers are usually fairly secretive with their parents about certain aspects of their lives and

Kim was no exception. However, during this time we were able to discover more – and it was not only from Kim herself. The support she received was truly inspiring and it was often through these people that we learned about the deeply caring and compassionate person that she was.

She also had an influence on the Hospital and Hospice staff who were involved with her. She made the effort to remember everyone's name and was always smiling and appreciative of what they were doing to help her. For three years, on the anniversary of Kim's death, we took flowers to the staff of the hospice where she died. They always remembered her and often commented on the caring influence she had had on their lives – there is a lesson for many of us here.

We have also realised and no longer believe that there is going to be that storybook occasion when all the pain and anger and other turbulent and ungovernable emotions are somehow going to erupt in a healing storm of tears and that, after that, grief will give way to calm acceptance. It is just not going to happen. Acknowledging this is has been a major step for all of us.

The inevitable result of this monumental event in our lives was that, like others before and after us, we were compelled to start soul searching; to try to decide what "it" is, indeed, all about and to redefine our priorities to correspond with the people we had suddenly become.

One of the first critical lessons was that there are some things that you can change and some that you can't. In some situations (Kim's illness and the total helplessness we felt) there was absolutely nothing we could have done. At that time, in our lives and circumstances, with science and medicine as they were, with the very best will in the world, it wouldn't have mattered what we'd done or how much money we'd spent, it would have changed nothing and the result would have been the same.

This goes for people also – there are some who you believe will never change and it is up to you as to how you handle them. There is only your own formula for doing this. Those who are constantly negative, sarcastic, deceitful, conniving, cunning, cynical, manipulative, slow to help and praise and encourage others are those who, quite probably, have big personal issues and challenges and are unhappy within themselves and unlikely to change - unless they realise themselves the unhappiness in their own lives and the influence they have on those around them. Do they need to experience a life changing personal tragedy to wake up? I hope not as that is not something to wish on anybody.

The positivity that we prefer extends to those around us in the workplace and at home. One of the most beneficial lessons I learned is to believe in the best of human nature and people's abilities. If I had to do some counting I can confidently say that this has worked far more often than it has not. The merit of approaching others in this way is that it is immensely rewarding and it usually brings out the best in others.

This could be middle age rearing its head, but my memory seems to be far shorter for things that are not relevant. At whatever meetings, social gatherings or discussions that I attend it is as though my mind absorbs whatever is necessary, discards the rest and then goes one step further. It then decides if there is a lesson to be learned from the meeting and then this is stored for future access. The other details and memories are still there but their level of importance has reduced considerably. It is as though my mind is telling me to listen, keep what is important, learn – and move on.

What I have found helpful over time is trying to speak to and help others who have lived through a tragic loss.

If we hear of some family that has recently lost a child, and only if it is not intrusive, we send them a letter, based on my Compassionate Friends presentation, that is for them to read if they wish.
The timing of this is important. Only once the full reality of the death has set in can we send the letter because, during

any time before this, usually the bereaved are too numb to be open to any form of suggestion and outside help, particularly from someone they do not know. Also, this is usually done impersonally by fax or e-mail after some brief initial contact. Many of those who have lost someone for the first time do not expect anybody to actually understand what they are going through and this is right, because each person's loss is unique and very special to them and this loss and the way that it happened will carry unique aspects that nobody else will understand, even though they might have been through a loss themselves.

After they have read the letter, and should they so choose, we then visit the bereaved and help in whatever way we can. Usually this is at their home as it is the most comfortable for them and we sit and talk about the loss, what happened and how they are feeling. What is important to understand at this point is that the bereaved often want to talk about what happened and what they are feeling and one of the most important aspects of this time is to be an extremely patient and compassionate listener.

With our also having been through a loss there is an immediate affinity and often the conversation flows freely, even the first time that we meet. There is usually an almost tangible bond that is forged between those who have gone through this experience – simply because we understand and there is so much that does not need to be said. We start with the awful understanding that we are members of the worst club in the world which carries a lifetime membership and it is then dependent upon each situation as to how the relationship progresses.

Because the association is more supportive than social, it tends to be short-lived, lasting only until they feel more able to cope with everyday life.

On a day-to-day basis we try to live according to what we have learned and I'm also very aware that an important part of my life now is a constant search for total understanding and acceptance of what happened to our family.

Of course, I have no guarantee that there will come a day when everything will fall into place but I believe this kind of insight is worth striving for regardless as, at the very least, it is a journey heading for a goal we would all like to achieve: inner peace.

Some Words for the Bereaved

Words cannot describe what you feel when the full realisation of what has happened hits you.

Unfortunately there is no recipe or formula to magically fix the pain of what you are going through and time is the best healer but once the initial shock and bewilderment has passed there are some important factors that bear consideration.

No matter how much time has passed there are still going to be occasions when your resilience is sorely tested.

You are going to be faced with vulnerable and poignant 'trigger times' when something will spark a vivid memory of your departed which brings with it an equally intense emotional reaction. The obvious triggers are birthdays and anniversaries – but there is a whole host of other triggers that might be totally unexpected that can cause a painful reaction.

Certain sights, sounds, series of events, smells, foods and many other situations can cause this to happen and, in many cases, they take you by surprise.

For example, in some public conveniences in shopping malls the paper towel dispensers are the same as the one in Kim's room at the Hospice. The first time I came across one of these after the funeral caused a rush of painful memories of Kim's suffering and my day changed completely after that.

Don't expect that anyone who has not lived through an experience like this will understand what you are going through. It is inevitable that those around you are going to make mistakes and say and do the wrong thing at times. For the most part, the actions and words of these people arise from genuine feelings of sadness and compassion and are being expressed in the sincerest way that they know how. Some don't know what to say and so say nothing at all and others may even avoid you for just that reason.

If anyone causes awkwardness or offence, it's probably not intentional and it is up to you to realise this and handle the situation gracefully, tactfully, diplomatically and with dignity.

Human nature being what it is, it's quite possible that you may be affected by a sense of inadequacy. You may question the way that you are grieving, compare yourself with others in the family and think that the others are 'grieving better' as they appear to be handling situations more competently, appearing to be more conscious of others in the family and are more caring and so on.

The bottom line is that you are the person you are with your own responses and reactions. Whilst doing your best to do your best, this is not the time to try being someone you are not. Without honesty and authenticity your grieving process will be hindered or even blocked. You owe it to yourself and those around you to heal as thoroughly and healthily as you can.

There is usually a marked difference in the way of grieving between the sexes. We all have emotions but there is a difference in the way that they are handled. Females are generally more directly in touch with their emotions and will usually be far more open and prepared to talk and release their emotions than males.

Females will often talk to bring others closer, while males are afraid of showing their emotions, often due to the 'tough guy' stereotypes they have been brought up to believe in and, if males do expose their emotions and are then hurt in some way, then they will tend to hold themselves back in future – if you are not exposed, you can't get hurt!

Many, if not most, support groups for the bereaved will have more women than men attending them. It is just the way that it is. My observations on "Men and Grieving" is further on.

Life will never be the same but you have an important choice to make. There could come a time when you examine yourself, your purpose and those around you and you decide to set a more carefully considered direction for your life.

Please beware of the trap of having your tragic experience influence your life negatively. It is all too easy to view your life as now being stripped of any opportunities and good experiences that could come your way. Managing a changed life is difficult enough without the added burden of believing that what has happened has taken away anything that could possibly be positive now and in the future. This energy sapping mindset is focused on weakness, feeds on itself and drains you and those around you.

Try not to allow what has happened to dominate your thinking and try as often as possible to be aware of what you are thinking about and the way that you are thinking – positive or negative – with the goal of breaking the negative thought habits.

There is a subtle but great difference between self pity and grieving and feeling sad and it takes a conscious effort to recognise this. It takes practice but the answer is to be conscious of every time that you do it and reward and encourage yourself for every small positive step.

What also helps is changing the way you express yourself, speaking in the present tense about life and, when you are genuinely ready, talking to others positively and briefly about the progress you are making.

The healing process takes courage and there are and always will be times when your emotions are intense, the mental images sharp and clear and the memories painful and it is up to you to conduct yourself in the most dignified way you can.

You owe it to yourself, to those around you and to the memory of your lost one.

THE GRIEVING PROCESS AND HOW TO HELP A GRIEVING FAMILY

The words which follow are not intended to disrupt nor interfere with any established social and religious norms and customs. Many of these rituals have been initiated over centuries with good and solid reasons behind them and they often provide a measure of comfort, reason and order in a mind-numbing situation for the bereaved. Also, although I have focused on our situation with Kim, grieving is not restricted to when a loved one has died. A divorce, the loss of a job, emigrating to another country - all involve upheaval and change and discomfort and can involve grief to some degree.

How It Feels

As I have mentioned, it is important to realise that because we are all different people we will all show our grief differently and that some of these ways might be seen as surprising and even disturbing. It is also important to understand that when you are in this kind of shock you often can't tell how you are going to react to different situations and it is ultimately each person's common sense that will determine how they behave. We have learned that any 'unusual' behaviour tends to emerge when just the immediate family or nobody else is around. For example, I weeded the garden or tidied my workshop when I couldn't sleep at night and I know of someone who visited their child's grave at all hours of the night. These activities are not offensive or intrusive but they would definitely appear out of the ordinary to a casual observer.

When your mind and your heart seem incapable of getting any sense out of anything, when there seem to be no answers, direction or solace, you could quite well feel compelled to do something physical that is mindless, repetitive or habitual in an effort to allay these feelings to some extent. Perhaps this kind of behaviour is prompted by the subconscious to gently re-introduce the process of restoring order amongst overwhelming chaos or even just to help us re-discover the basic rhythms that underlie day-today life; whatever the cause, this kind of activity can fulfil a need and provide a small sense of accomplishment that can be very valuable at a time like this.

Right after Kim's death and funeral there was no solace that anyone could give and we operated on 'auto-pilot' and were numb to everything around us. Overridden by a feeling of total helplessness, we didn't know what to think, to feel, to eat and when to sleep. Time meant nothing and we tried desperately to get some sense of our new situation and reality. During this intense time we mostly did not wish to be sociable – we needed time by ourselves to come to terms with what had happened and to try to know and decide what to do next.

What did help was receiving mobile 'phone text messages just letting us know that people were thinking of us – and with offers of help if we needed it. We could then reply or 'phone as and when we could. If the 'phone rang, sometimes we did not answer as we just did not feel like it. At this time we were experiencing a whole range of emotions which were confusing. Fortunately we were surrounded by very thoughtful friends and relatives who helped with day to day chores and provided easily prepared meals.

After the reality of Kim's passing sank in, then the reactions started to emerge – more tears, anger, questioning and more; this is the second intense period when emotions and the intellect are very busy and often in conflict. This is when some common sense and a degree of normality are re-establishing themselves but, at the same time, trying to accommodate and conflicting with the new reality.

Some Advice on Dealing with the Bereaved

It is difficult to know what to do and say to a person who has just lost someone very close to them. There are the socially and culturally accepted practices which definitely have their meaningful place but, for example, how do you react when a colleague has just returned to work after the funeral?
What do you say?

How do you react?

Many people have asked us just these questions.

There are many factors which need to be taken into account and sensitively understood when you are "an outsider" faced with this situation.

YOUR APPROACH

With the best will in the world, as a colleague, friend or even relative you can have little real understanding of what a bereaved person has been through and compassion is what is required at this time. It is also a time to be subtle and gentle and to do things that are helpful – but without making the person feel helpless or trying to make them deviate from their normal day to day routine. Helping with part of the workload is the most obvious thing to do and there are small, helpful, gestures, such as making a cup of tea, which are a little way of saying that you care and are concerned.

It is probably better to 'do' rather than to 'say' as so many people do not know what to say and what comes out can often be interpreted as being too 'light' or too 'heavy'.

To a large extent, the circumstances of each death will also dictate the way in which the bereaved will behave. For example, imagine a person losing someone suddenly or perhaps in a violent or perhaps senselessly violent way. Besides trying to come to terms with the confusion of loss and helplessness and anger, they could be suffering from deep feelings of guilt and / or remorse over what happened. Not surprisingly, they could feel totally inconsolable at times.

WHERE ANGELS FEAR TO TREAD

This could not be the time to invite the bereaved out to have some fun and 'forget' what they have been through. This aspect needs to be handled extremely sensitively with the overall understanding that the bereaved are never going to forget. Again, different personalities will react differently, but do not be surprised if a family with a recent loss does not wish to be sociable.

Please think carefully before asking questions such as:-

"Are you feeling better now?" – this is something you never feel better about, you learn how to cope better.

"Are you over the loss now?" – this kind of tragedy you are never over.

This second question appears to be asked after a certain fixed time period and I have no idea who has drawn this timetable up. It seems as though around three months is the timing for the first question, and around nine months and after for the second.

Also, please think before saying things such as:-

"It was God's will",

"It was a good way to die",

"Count your blessings",

"God has just gained a wonderful angel",

"Think of your wonderful memories",

"There are others who are worse off than you",

"You had some wonderful years together",

"Try and put it behind you and get on with your life"

- and that whoever has died "is in heaven and at peace", are not things that the recently bereaved want to hear.

Possibly the most grating comment of all is "The Lord giveth and the Lord taketh away." The bereaved are hurt, confused and angry at their God and the world and clichés like this do not help the situation even though they may be well meaning and intended to be comforting.

Grieving people need to know that you are aware that they are experiencing a very unique pain that you just can't understand. Quite possibly, they won't be able to control or hide their feelings of helplessness, frustration and despair. They will find it comforting and very helpful if you make it clear that it is completely acceptable if they need to break down and that you will be a willing shoulder to cry on and an ear to listen – providing quiet support as long as they need it.

What is important is that the bereaved should be aware that there is a constant support base around them and they have to know this in subtle ways – an easily prepared meal left at the home or brought to work, a 'phone text message, helping with shopping, sending a particularly well worded and appropriate card are some examples.

Unless the situation really demands it don't try to take over a household. Those in the house have enough on their minds, are probably more than comfortable with things the way they are and are likely to be upset even more by someone trying to take over what is, for the moment, a very liveable and handle-able situation – one of the few areas of their world that is predictable and under their control.

There is another aspect that may be quite difficult to understand. People who have lost immediate family do not initially wish to hear about some distant relative or friend of yours who has died at some time in the past. Their pain is their immediate pain that they are feeling right now. The feelings attached to a loss that is more remote are obviously just not as intense and, unless there is some very special relevance, the bereaved can only partly identify with this situation and mentioning it could increase the load they are already carrying.

I might be sticking my neck out quite far here, but if someone who has suffered a loss needs some form of counselling or therapy, surely that should be provided by someone who is suitably qualified - and who has also suffered a loss. You can have all the training and qualifications in the world but, unless you have been through at least something similar to the person who is coming to you for help, it is extremely difficult to understand and empathise with them and to counsel appropriately.

LETTER – "THE LOSS OF A CHILD - ONE FAMILY'S EXPERIENCE"

We feel desperate for you and your grief, particularly if this is something new and fresh for you – please know that our family understands and the reason I am sending this to you is just to relate the experience and observations we had as a family and, even though everyone is unique and your loss is unique, hopefully what we went through will help you to come to terms with your own grief and give you some sense of understanding and direction.

We lost our eighteen year old daughter, Kim, to rampant cancer (Melanoma) in January 2003 and, if it is possible to understand this, we have considered ourselves to be a fortunate family with what has happened to us. Believe me, the experience we went through was devastating – I don't have to tell you this – and there are still times when the whole horror seems like a dream, but, given what we went through, we believe that we did the right things at the right times and we were incredibly fortunate in having the most wonderful support base around us – family, friends, Kim's friends, her school and Chaplain were magnificent, our neighbourhood was incredible. People we didn't know were aware of our situation and were and still are so giving and understanding – amazing!!

We were also lucky to be told about The Compassionate Friends (www.compassionatefriends.org) and we all had private sessions with the counsellors. Wonderful people - and I think the best part of the experience was that we found they were people who were prepared to listen – guide us in the right direction with careful questions – but really listen!!

From our counselling and over time we have learned 3 things:-

1) This pain that you are feeling now is never going to go away – it hasn't for us. However, it will diminish with time and you will learn how to handle it better!!

2) It is OK to have "Me" time – maybe there are times when you just don't feel like communicating or going out, or going to work. That's OK – it's part of the process and, within reason, everyone is entitled - and needs - to take time and try and understand and come to terms with their grief and new situation.

3) Everybody needs to respect each other's way of grieving – it is different for everybody and every personality handles it their own way. For example:-

Our surviving daughter, who was 16 at the time, withdrew and grieved privately (and still does). She then went back to school and really tried – but there were many memories there for her and she, in effect, lost the first two terms of her schooling that year. Her biggest battle was to get any of her friends and colleagues to understand how she felt and what she was trying to get to grips with. She is also now our only child and this is difficult for her. She and Kim were normal teenagers and bickering and fighting was not unusual – however, she suddenly didn't have anyone, even to fight with!! This has been a big adjustment and maturing time for her.

Kim's mother – and I believe it has to be hardest for the mother – withdrew for a few months, concentrated on the family and could not speak to or relate to anybody who did not understand our situation.

She was a very angry person and, at times, she could not stand being in any form of public place and hated going to the supermarket, for example. It took time for her to get back to work and be more able to relate to people in general – however, she still has periods when the pain is intense.

Our domestic servant – bless her - who was so supportive and who has been with us since before Kim was born, also had a tough time and has had her moments. A counselling session did wonders for her, her acceptance and her perspective.

And the dad?? Contrary to popular belief, cowboys DO cry and I have also had my moments – but my grief has also been a private one. The funeral was on a Thursday and I was back at work the following Monday – maybe because it was a constant in my life. I am fortunate in that I had a very supportive staff at work and, if I fell asleep during a meeting, they would quietly close the door and let me sleep until I woke up.

Coming to terms with my grief has been the hardest thing for me and I have spent many a long night trying to get my mind right and comfortable. I have also been known to weed the garden at 2 o'clock in the morning!!

So, we all experienced and are handling the same loss and sadness in different ways. I don't need to tell you that this is a life changing experience and we will never see things the same way ever again. Our perspectives and priorities have changed – I believe for the better – and it is very sad that we needed to live through something like this in order to become more aware, better and more caring people.

Strange triggers have reopened the wound and different memories and situations have affected us in different ways. Sights, sounds and smells have taken on a different meaning – my big trigger is music and I have spent many an hour listening to words and music with an intensity I never had before.

We also learned that it is not necessary to apologise if we broke down in some public place – we are who we are and grieving is definitely allowed. Anybody who isn't (and isn't prepared to be) empathetic, compassionate and understanding is probably not worth knowing or associating with anyway!!

At times we have all wanted to talk so that we could understand and come to terms with our loss. However, we did find many people in our circle who were extremely uncomfortable discussing our situation – trying to change the subject, relating our experience to some distant relative of theirs etc. etc. We found that, ultimately, it was up to us to understand and move on – people who haven't been through what we have just don't know the kind of process we're trying to get through and it is unfair for us to expect them to be able to relate. The trick is to accept these situations graciously.

I think the most difficult times have been when we have individually had a "moment" or a "wobbly", wanted to share the feelings and there has been nobody around who understands – this has been the most trying experience of all.

As I said, I think we were fortunate in this tragic situation. In addition to having an amazing support base around us, Kim lasted close to three months after her diagnosis and we were able to speak to her, discuss things openly – as this is the way she wanted it – appreciate having her around, be able to say "goodbye" and reach some degree of closure.

In essence, I am saying that we all communicated at all times. Yes, we each had our private moments, but, during Kim's ordeal, at the end of every day we sat and discussed what we were doing, what direction we were going in, what the Oncologist was saying, should we be doing something different, or more - and so on and so on.

After the funeral we sat again, once our friends and family had left our home, and asked ourselves if there was anything else we could have done, or anything we could have done differently. We could honestly say that there was nothing that we could have or wanted to change. So – from that we knew that we had no feelings of guilt, remorse or responsibility for Kim's death.
Some things you cannot change and we knew then that what we are missing and will always miss is her presence.

If I can offer any advice it is to ask you to try and ensure that you are at peace with yourself and that your family and support structure (whatever that is) is strong. Family, relationship or work issues are definitely not a part of this process and communicate as best you can with the right people all the time. I believe that you can then be comfortable that you are grieving for the right reasons.

Try and get past all guilt, remorse and feelings of responsibility for the death – whoever you have lost has gone to a better place. We believe that totally and have had experiences that have convinced us of this.

Some examples:-

On the afternoon of Kim's death she was very aware of a presence at the foot of her bed - which she wanted to go away – this girl fought right until the end!! The strength that she displayed at that stage was totally contrary to her condition – she was weak, emaciated and could hardly breathe, yet she held me with incredible intensity. We believe that this presence was there to help her over to the other side – and that her spirit left her body at this point. After this episode Kim became totally unresponsive and she then left us a few hours later.

A few days after Kim's death my wife was dozing in Kim's room when she felt two hands gently in the palms of her hands and she felt a strong, peaceful and loving presence in the room. There have been other instances, as she is particularly sensitive to Kim, and she also regularly smells a perfume that Kim loved.

On Kim's birthday in the September after her death, I happened to be on a flight between London and New York – fortunate to have 3 seats to myself – and I was lying with my eyes closed when white, grey and black clouds moved in front of me. I have no idea how long this took, but they formed themselves into Kim's face – beautiful, smiling and peaceful.

Please make of these incidents what you will – but they were very meaningful and consoling for us.

Please also decide what kind of relationship you would like to have with your lost one. We do believe that Kim is still around us and we talk to her regularly – each in our own private way. I believe that we should have a healthy and caring time when we communicate with the departed – and that they still have a sense of humour – being too serious with Kim makes me uncomfortable.

However, there are times to be serious and I had a long chat with her on the first anniversary of her passing. That day we visited her oncologist and the Hospice, taking flowers for the people who had been so wonderful and caring. The staff at the Hospice told us about a 17 year old girl who was in the same situation – she was on her way out and had hours to live. After speaking to the parents we left and, on the way home, I asked Kim to please help this young girl in whatever way she could.

And that is basically our story – the lessons we have learned are enormous and we also learned that, at the end of the day, we all need to conduct ourselves with dignity. This experience is incredibly painful – and, yet, life goes on!! Bills still need to be paid and there are family and friends to be looked after, developed and maybe get to know again.

We try always to remember what we have learned and still will learn from our experience – however painful it has been – we have become better people for it.

And please never forget that your life begins and continues from this moment on!!

MEN AND GRIEVING

This is the transcript of a presentation I gave at a meeting of The Compassionate Friends as I was concerned that so few men appeared to feel that they would not benefit from some form of positive counselling. So I did some reading and research and this is the result. Maybe you will see the former teacher in me!

Men, their emotions and their way of dealing with and showing feelings to those around them is, I think, something worth understanding – and particularly so in tragic situations such the one my family lived through, where the world as we know it is suddenly turned upside down and life becomes a different experience. After a major tragedy we all sooner or later come to the realisation that we are going to be living our lives differently, with a new perspective and outlook which, hopefully, will be more positive and loving to both ourselves and those around us.

But how do we handle this process of grieving and reach this goal of a new understanding? When struggling through this kind of tragedy, not only do both sexes have to deal with the same hurt, pain, bewilderment, helplessness and all the rest of those emotions, they then have to try to make some sense of it all and rebuild lives of acceptance and greater awareness.

I have seen a few instances where relationships have stumbled and even fallen apart because of:-

First - a lack of communication. All of us need to feel that we can talk freely, deeply and meaningfully to those closest to us without fear of judgement. Surely when one has to live through a tragedy on this scale there is at least some comfort in feeling able to trust others with your innermost feelings?

Second - a lack of understanding that we all grieve in different ways and that, within reason everyone needs to be allowed to find their own way of living through their own process. Everyone is different and so handles any situation differently and with a different time span. Trying to force anyone through this process is going to be counterproductive – we each arrive at our destination of realisation at our own pace.

Third – blame. Guilt is perhaps the hardest of all emotions to deal with. Some people, unable to manage it, displace the 'blame' for their loved one's passing onto their partner or some other 'convenient' person. Because this blame can never be acknowledged – because it might be refuted – its' toxic effects can seriously damage a relationship, especially if it is the coping mechanism of both partners.

Directly related to this is the fact that men and women are different in the way they handle and express emotions – they just are!! I hope that what I am saying and am about to say does not come across as a lecture – that is not the intention - but I have done some reading over the past few months and will be quoting from those who have dedicated a considerable amount of quality time to researching this topic. For example, studies have shown that men rate just as high as women in emotional awareness and, with married couples, husbands proved as attuned to their mates' stress levels as their wives – and just as capable of offering support. So, we all experience the same emotions with the same degree of intensity - but we process them differently.

Dr. Josh Coleman, who wrote "The Lazy Husband" says that: "Emotions live in the background of a man's life and the foreground of a woman's. Testosterone affects feelings in men, who compartmentalise and intellectualise more. Women seem naturally more in touch with their emotions, while men have to work at it."

Dr. John Gray, the author of "Men Are From Mars, Women Are From Venus" agrees and says that in times of trauma or decision, men disappear into their individual emotional 'caves' and will only reappear emotionally when they have worked through their situation and come up with an acceptable solution.

This is naturally difficult for a woman to understand, particularly when women are sensitive to feeling rejected when they don't get the attention they need. How do you handle a situation when the woman wants to talk through what she is feeling and the man has gone into his mental 'cave' to work out his solution. This calls for a whole lot of understanding and consideration on both sides.

So, what is behind this strong and silent mask that men present?

A man's deepest fear is that he is not good at what he is doing – that he is not good enough.

Psychiatrist, Dr. Mark Goulston, says that it all boils down to vulnerability and that: "women talk to clear their heads but men think before they talk. If they didn't, they would risk saying something stupid and being humiliated or offending another man and being beaten up. They are safer not saying anything. Most men are far more insecure than they like to admit – and more so than their wives ever guess!!

"Inside every man is a secret fear that that he lacks competence and courage, that he is not as manly as he should be. A man knows he is supposed to take complete care of his family and to fix whatever gets broken. When he is feeling powerless, he shuts down and withdraws because he is afraid that, if he gives emotions an inch, they will take a mile."

Traditionally, men have been brought up not to expose their anxieties and to believe that it is not manly to open up emotionally. These lessons begin early.

By the age of one, boys make less eye contact than girls and pay more attention to moving objects, like cars, than to human faces. Both mothers and fathers talk less about feelings (except anger) to sons than daughters and boys' vocabularies include fewer words that describe feelings.

Later, at home and at school, boys learn to choke back tears and show no fear. A naval graduate reacted with surprise on seeing his father shed a tear at his graduation ceremony. He had learned to eat fast, talk loud, compete ferociously and keep his feelings under guard. "Showing emotion," he said, "is a no-can-do among men."

As boys grow, faces once as openly emotional as those of girls, become less expressive and, as adults, men use fewer words and they tend to talk as a means of putting themselves in a 'one up' situation, helping to combat their feeling of vulnerability. This is contrary to women who usually talk to draw others closer.

The biggest lesson to be learned from this is to understand the man's feeling of vulnerability and lack of control. This is especially important when partners try to discuss a common family situation or problem.

When the wife gives vent to her feelings that is just what she is doing – venting her feelings. This helps her to work through what she is experiencing in a situation where she just wants someone to listen to her without being judgemental and who accepts her for who she is and the range of emotions she is experiencing.

Because a man is brought up to believe that his role is to fix things, his way of approaching the situation is to offer suggestions and solutions – and this is exactly what the wife is not looking for! She just wants to let everything out knowing that she is going to be listened to and accepted and loved for who she is.

So, the husband, because of the way that his mind works, believes that he is being helpful by offering answers and then cannot understand why this is not what his wife is looking for. The husband's reaction is then to get upset or withdraw as he feels that he and his solutions are not being accepted and his own vulnerability is being further exposed.
She talks until she finds the answer, he finds the answer and then talks about it.

And so the male emotional spiral becomes more intense and more incomprehensible to the female and this is compounded as John Gray describes: "Ironically, when a man really cares a lot, his fear of failure increases and he then gives less! To avoid failure he stops giving to the people he wants to give to the most! When a man is insecure he may compensate by not caring about anybody but himself and his most automatic defense response is to say: 'I don't care'."

How to fix this from the man's perspective?

John Gray says further that: "The first step for a man in learning how to give and release is to realise that it is OK to make mistakes and it is OK to fail and that he doesn't have to have all the answers."

He then comes to realise that "when he doesn't deliver he is still adequate and still deserves love and appreciation for doing his best. He does not condemn himself because he knows he is not perfect and that he is always doing his best and his best is good enough. He is able to apologise for his mistakes because he expects forgiveness, love and appreciation for doing his best."

Easily said and not so easily done! There is a massive load of upbringing, tradition and baggage to understand and overcome – and now it needs to be learned after a life-changing tragedy!! However, we all need to start somewhere and mutual understanding and acceptance is a good base to work from.

This is not meant as an apology for men – nor does it mean that the man's way is the correct way of handling tragic situations. Men just react differently, will withdraw rather than let their feelings be exposed and will not let their vulnerability show. Men will often not admit to having any sort of problem. Women are far more open to exposing themselves emotionally and talking freely. It is a way of letting emotions run, drawing support without any fear and so understanding and coming to terms with a new situation.

Men are made differently and usually have a problem with this.

Dr. Elizabeth Levang has written a book called: "When Men Grieve: Why Men Grieve Differently and How You Can Help" which I found very helpful and she describes six stages that we go through – we all go through them, but her focus is on men and how these emotions are perceived and I am quoting freely from her book:-

DENIAL

Initially we often feel immobilized by death or a loss – as if time is standing still. Denial is a normal reaction to a major upheaval – it helps both men and women handle the stress of everyday living by preserving or protecting their sense of self worth. While women feel engulfed by riotous emotions and want support and some assurance that the pain will not last forever, they usually feel comfortable talking through their pain and the struggle of where to begin to describe the enormity of their sorrow.

Men, however, are conditioned to control life and they feel that they must go on in the face of tragedy, appearing unemotional and content to carry their own burdens. Many men seem unwilling to face grief squarely in the eye. They feel they can best deal with the situation by avoiding it – hoping that the grief will ease and disappear naturally with time.

Men have learned from experience to push sensitive or painful issues out of their awareness – what is out of mind is under control. To express feelings would be humiliating an admission of defeat. The hard part of this is that vigilantly repressing emotions is a huge task and the tension can become enormous, with few options for releasing that tension.

So, the grief is compartmentalized and blocked out of their conscious mind and great effort is given to carrying on with life and keeping busy. Keeping active and preoccupied is what is needed. It's not that the death has had no effect. On the contrary, its effect is so great that men feel bound to reject reality and deny their emotions in order to cope with the situation. For men, denial is not an unwillingness to grieve, but a strategy for grieving and men would have no reason to be in denial if their loss did not matter.

ANGER

While an angry woman tends to be looked upon by society as emotionally unstable and unfeminine, an angry man tends to be looked upon as having strength of character and moral conviction. Women can be angry in their grief too – but the taboos and stereotypes against anger leave many women feeling misunderstood and unsupported and their churning emotions may be interpreted as irritability and hostility.

But anger is one of the few emotions society readily allows men to possess and express and often it is a sign of virility and manhood. Society traditionally accepts men's' anger and it is seen as an entitlement that is both necessary and legitimate and so it should come as no surprise to see men displaying anger when grieving.

For men, anger helps even the odds. Submitting to grief is admitting that you have lost control of your life, your family and even yourself. Your anger shows that you have stood up to this grieving challenge and you are using it as a shield and a weapon.

Men know that there is energy and power in anger. When it races through them, they feel alive, empowered and forceful and the fact that anger demands attention helps some regain a degree of control over their lives. Men feel as if they are actively doing something and not just waiting to be ambushed by grief. Anger is not passive – it reassures men that they are not helpless, that they can make progress and perhaps even move ahead in their grieving. It protects, it camouflages, it gives a sense of control and sometimes it is a beginning of healing – a mechanism for coping and externally releasing some of what is brewing inside.

The trick is to ensure that the use of anger is healthy and realistic!!

Also, for anyone to react to an angry outburst seldom achieves results as this emotion is seldom rational. Hurling back insults and accusations, crying, slamming doors and giving the silent treatment only add salt to the wound.

However, addressing it head on and responding carefully to it with the understanding that hurt, frustration and insecurity are the underlying emotions is far more likely to obtain results.

CONTROL

The idea that we might somehow be to blame for our loss is both shocking and frightening and our integrity, honour and values are put at stake. And, if we are not to blame, then some outside force is and our tragedy has resulted from events beyond our control – or from our own poor judgement and inadequacies. We can come to believe that we have failed to control either our environment or our own lives.

Men are expected to be in control – in all situations and at all times, whether at home, work or in a social environment. Men believe that they must not show weakness of any kind, or be overly dependent on others for support, advice or encouragement. They are encouraged to be dominant, aggressive, powerful and capable and, if men don't have the answer, they are supposed to know where and how to find it.

Although women are neither dependant nor helpless, many don't seem to have the same problem- solving drive or need to prove themselves that men have. Women are generally more flexible about how they face problems, even though they want things to go smoothly and grief is an intensely personal but also a relational challenge. Most want others to grieve with them and also to be comforted and understood – working co-operatively to process feelings, hurts and disappointments.

But, being a man is about being brave! Traditionally, a man is expected to protect and provide for his family and, if he or his family has been harmed by grief, he may feel that he has failed in his traditional role. So, some men assume the role of manager and attempt to make up for their failure by diligently trying to fix everyone and everything. They listen, support, comfort and empathise – pushing their own pain to the background to accomplish the task at hand. Their thinking is, if they can get everything in their family under control, they can then restore harmony and re-establish their role as family guardian. If possible, they would willingly transfer all their family's pain, heartache and suffering onto themselves.

Men also define themselves by the kind of work that they do and working harder and longer than others is a tried and tested way of affirming that they are competent, responsible and self reliant at work. Therefore their moral strength and character will be affirmed if they can appear strong and unfazed in front of their co-workers.

This admiration ensures status and respect – just the things that grief tries to wipe out! So, in addition to being a place of escape, men see that their job can also be a safe and legitimate place to work out aggression and anger about the world and its unjustness.

Yes, men do sometimes seek ways to escape the home, because it holds too many reminders of what has been lost – not just the tragedy, but the home does not appear to be the showplace of competence and the place of pride and honour that it once was.

So, work may take on a new intensity, leisure activities can take on a new importance, a new hobby might be started, a civic group or professional organization might be joined – but what is done is not nearly as important as the fact of doing something and doing it well. Activities organise, structure and concentrate men's' time and thoughts. They are an effective way to occupy time and, in the process, distract men from their grief and pain. Some men may even challenge themselves in daring and dangerous ways – all men want to find a way to ensure that bad things will stop happening to them and to those that they love and care about. By getting their life under control, they believe that they have bought the best insurance policy available.

BITTERNESS

Most of the time we expect our lives to be predictable, equitable and relatively uncomplicated and these normal expectations make us feel more secure, diminish our fears and increase our sense of satisfaction when what we anticipated has gone to plan.

But this tragedy has taught us that there are no guarantees in life – and now we have to accept that life is uncontrollable. This is not easy for either men or women and, generally, when that sense of predictability and security has been shattered, it is easy for bitterness to settle in. Bitterness is an elusive emotion – it is fermented anger and it is often expressed as sarcasm, resignation and/or resentment.
Many people feel they have been unfairly victimized and lament over why the death occurred and wonder if they might have brought the tragedy upon themselves. Comparing their lives with others, they may feel disappointed and that they have been singled out for disaster.

Bitterness, in a way, is about feeling ashamed – the way life was expected to go and the way it has turned out shakes self respect and self identity. The reaction from both men and women is: "I am ashamed that I did not foresee or plan for what has happened!"

In addition, men (as well as women) resent grief for trying to wrong and injure them and they feel insulted by the pain and suffering forced upon them and those they love. And so men set out to find a rational explanation as to why all this has happened. Men reject the notion of being a victim and they want to know what rule they broke or how they fell out of favour with the world – and when they discover that there is no rational explanation it is easy for a sense of hate and bitterness to develop.

Men can also feel shame if they feel that they are not living up to their partner's standards of good grieving. Sometimes they are accused of being in denial about emotional pain and that they are avoiding the work of processing grief. Women can get discouraged and angered by men's silence and their unwillingness to discuss feelings openly; as a result, some women believe that men are insensitive and uncaring - and this can result in seemingly critical and shaming remarks.

These words and accusations can make men feel defective and painfully self-conscious. Caught in the dilemma of maintaining their masculinity while trying to respect their partner's needs, many begin to feel embittered about the conflicting roles and expectations in their lives.

Though men feel they must be prepared to handle any adversity, this tragedy is a 'curved ball' and, consciously or unconsciously, they are indignant about the extreme emotional distress that accompanies grief – the unfairness is incomprehensible! Men feel they must avoid grief and disappointment and bitter feelings are a way to push away the hurt.

This is a time for determination and compassion from all involved!!

ADDICTIVE BEHAVIOURS

This is for all of us and I don't think that I need spend too much time here as I believe that we are all aware of the dangers.

Grief packs a serious punch and we should all realise that any attempt at denying the intensity or duration of grief is unlikely to be successful over time. Many of us become increasingly desperate when our usual range of stress reducing behaviours fails or when our emotional problems continue to escalate - and, to diminish the pain, some men and women turn to a range of addictive behaviours as a coping strategy. Some see alcohol as a way of anaesthetising their pain, while others escape into an extra-marital affair. The motivation is the same – find some outside diversion to occupy the mind and avoid the dismal work of grieving.

Unfortunately, today's society has often been labelled an addictive society because so many people rely on substances or activities to manage their stress and emotional pain. Alcohol, drugs, food, sex, gambling, work and exercising can all become components of addictive behaviour.

Taking this route is a substitute for reality, for intimacy and for healing. The momentary high we gain from winning at gambling or working out hard at the gym can seem unnaturally good when compared with the drudgery of grieving. The diversion is exciting, the relief feels good and, for a while, forgotten are the memories that have caused such pain.

Addictions and addictive behaviours are empty sources of pleasure and they are incapable of sustaining us physically, emotionally, intellectually and spiritually over any length of time. Anyone who tries to manage their grief by engaging in anything addictive runs the risk of becoming ensnared in the vicious cycle of addiction – a far greater problem than the one they are trying to solve!!

DESPAIR

All of us want to know that our life counts for something. We also all need some reinforcement that we contribute to the world in a significant way and having meaning in life helps us feel satisfied and secure with ourselves and those around us. Our own meaning of life comes when we review all the moments of our lives – the joyful and fulfilling moments, as well as the painful and disheartening times – and so much of the meaning we make is shaped by our interaction with others. Being part of our society and culture helps us learn our values, which shape who we are and how we act.

Values help our clarity and sense of purpose and personal tragedy feels like a sudden and incomprehensible violation of our value system. There is no simple explanation for why a tragedy occurs and we don't know in advance how we are going to react when tragedy strikes. An unexpected loss can render our life's compass useless and leave us wandering in search of meaning and clarity - and therefore purpose.

Many men describe despair as a pervasive sense of darkness and, like bitterness, despair is marked by a slow descent into an emotional prison as men sense that their efforts to fight off grief are feeble and useless. As the grieving man descends, he is overcome with a tiredness of spirit and, sometimes, even speech becomes difficult. He feels apathetic, listless and inert and his identity begins to crumble. Men want and expect life to be coherent but, in the chaos that grief brings, there are few standards that men can use to measure and demonstrate their worth. So life can then change from challenge and opportunity to peril and fear, and trust in the world is then questioned.

As I have mentioned, in the struggle to understand what has happened to them, men isolate themselves emotionally and, if they believe that things will not improve, they may project a sense of calmness and resignation. While they may insist that nothing is wrong, inside these men are seething – and behind the façade of competence and normality there lurks a secret depression.

Depression for men and women is naturally common in grieving. However, men more than women feel that they must overcome the stigma of weakness associated with being depressed. Men are supposed to be invulnerable and, rather than admit this, many men, out of shame, avoid seeking help.

This also presents a dilemma for the partner – some women want to protect their partner by helping to keep his depression a secret. They minimize his low mood and give ready excuses to family and friends about his declining ability to function normally. Other women fear what their partner's depression means for the survival of their relationship and, afraid that confronting their partner will only make things worse, they help conceal the situation by saying nothing about it.

Ultimately despair directs us away from hope and towards self destruction. To climb out from this requires willpower, great courage and a conscious decision to work at getting better - to find new meaning and rediscover hope!

Healing starts when men begin to restore their relationships and work to establish a more functional identity – one that integrates their old self with their new self.

These different stages outline some scary scenarios but we will all live through them at some stage of our grieving process at our own level. My wish in outlining these is that hopefully we can all recognize them for what they are and realise that we are not unique in what we are experiencing and feeling.

Tragedies, such as the one we lived through, are life changing and understanding the grieving process is, I believe, essential so that we are better equipped to handle what life has thrown at us.

At times it might be hard to accept – but what we have lived through actually provides a wonderful opportunity for families to grow closer and to grow together with a better understanding of each other and a better perspective and approach to the world we live in.

What we need to do is communicate with each other with understanding - and with any siblings who are left behind, and all those others who are important to us.

Without communication barriers are thrown up and often resentment sets in and the basic family unit is threatened.

With communication hope can be rekindled and a new meaning and purpose to life can be created.

BIBLIOGRAPHY

"When Men Grieve: Why Men Grieve Differently and How You Can Help" – Elizabeth Levang, Ph.D

"Men Are From Mars, Women Are From Venus" – John Gray

Psychiatrist - Dr. Mark Goulston

"The Lazy Husband" – Dr. Josh Coleman

www.ingramcontent.com/pod-product-compliance
Lightning Source LLC
Chambersburg PA
CBHW071235280526
45787CB00002B/943